The Countries

Denmark

Tamara L. Britton
ABDO Publishing Company

visit us at
www.abdopub.com

Published by ABDO Publishing Company, 4940 Viking Drive, Edina, Minnesota 55435.
Copyright © 2004 by Abdo Consulting Group, Inc. International copyrights reserved in
all countries. No part of this book may be reproduced in any form without written
permission from the publisher.

Printed in the United States.

Photo Credits: Corbis pp. 5, 6, 9, 10, 11, 13, 14, 16, 19, 21, 22, 24, 26, 27, 29, 31, 33,
    34, 36; Getty Images pp. 18, 19, 30, 37

Editors: Kate A. Conley, Stephanie Hedlund, Kristianne E. Vieregger
Art Direction & Maps: Neil Klinepier

Library of Congress Cataloging-in-Publication Data

Britton, Tamara L., 1963-
    Denmark / Tamara L. Britton
        p. cm. -- (The countries)
    Includes index.
    Summary: An introduction to the history, geography, plants and animals, government,
people, and culture of Denmark.
    ISBN 1-59197-291-4
    1. Denmark--Juvenile literature. I. Title. II. Series.

DL109.B65 2003
948.9--dc21
                                                                    2003044314

Contents

Hej!

Hello from Denmark! Denmark is a **Scandinavian** country. It lies on a **peninsula**, but it also includes hundreds of islands.

Denmark's land is mainly flat. A long history of human **habitation** has hurt the plant and animal population. The country used to have many forests. But today, only one-tenth of the land is forested.

Denmark's government is a **constitutional monarchy**. It is ruled by a king or queen and a one-house **parliament**. Denmark's government and people work together to make sure all Danes are taken care of.

Denmark's people enjoy a high standard of living. Almost all Danes can read and write. Danes enjoy many social rights, such as housing and insurance. When they are not working, they like to read, visit museums, play sports, and spend time outdoors.

Hej *from Denmark!*

Fast Facts

OFFICIAL NAME: Kingdom of Denmark (Kongeriget Danmark)
CAPITAL: Copenhagen

LAND
- Area: 16,639 square miles (43,095 sq km)
- Highest Point: Yding Skovhøj 568 feet (173 m)
- Lowest Point: Lammefjord –23 feet (–7 m)
- Major River: Gudenå River
- Major Lake: Lake Arre

PEOPLE
- Population: 5,368,854 (July 2002 est.)
- Major Cities: Copenhagen, Århus, Odense, Ålborg
- Languages: Danish, English, German
- Religions: Lutheranism, Catholicism, Islam, Judaism

GOVERNMENT
- Form: Constitutional monarchy
- Head of State: Monarch
- Head of Government: Prime minister
- Legislature: Parliament called Folketing

ECONOMY
- Agricultural Products: Eggs, meats, dairy products; wheat, barley, sugar beets, potatoes
- Mining Products: None
- Manufactured Products: Food products, electronics, ships, machinery, furniture, china, silver products
- Money: Danish krone (1 Danish krone = 100 øre)

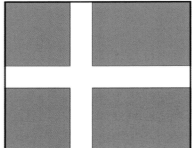

Denmark's flag

Danish kroner and øre

Timeline

400	Danes establish trade with Romans
700s	Danes repel Franks, establish Denmark's southern border
900	King Harald Bluetooth unites Danes
1016-1042	Danes rule England
1240	Civil wars begin to weaken Denmark
1397-1523	Union of Kalmar
1657-1660	Denmark and Sweden at war
1700-1720	Denmark fights Sweden to regain lost lands
1814	Denmark loses Norway to Sweden in Treaty of Kiel
1849	Denmark becomes parliamentary democracy
1940-1945	Germans occupy Denmark during World War II
1953	Danes draft a new constitution
2000	Danes vote against euro

Kingdom of Denmark

People have lived in Denmark for about 100,000 years. The nation's first residents were hunters and gatherers. Eventually, the people developed a more settled society based on agriculture. By 400, Danes had an established **culture**, and they were trading with the Romans.

In the 700s, the Franks were pushing northward. The Danes held back these invaders. They signed a treaty that made the Eider River Denmark's southern border.

Denmark's first king was Gorm the Old. Around 900, Gorm the Old's son, King Harald Bluetooth, united the people of Denmark. He also brought Christianity to the Danes.

During this time, Danish Vikings sailed throughout the region. They conquered many neighboring lands, including parts of Norway and Sweden. The Danes also ruled England from 1016 to 1042.

Danish influence and power continued to spread. By the 1200s, the Danes controlled the area along the Baltic Sea. But in 1240, **civil wars** began to break out. This weakened the country's influence in the area.

Vikings and their longboats were feared throughout Europe. This replica shows the longboat's length of 60 feet (18 m).

In 1375, a woman named Margaret ruled Denmark as **regent** for her young son. Over time, she also became Norway's regent and was elected to rule Sweden. In 1397, Queen Margaret united Denmark, Sweden, and Norway under the Union of Kalmar. Queen Margaret ruled all three countries until her death in 1412. The Union of Kalmar continued until Sweden became independent in 1523. Norway and Denmark remained united under one ruler.

Queen Margaret

In 1657, Sweden and Denmark went to war. Sweden took much Danish and Norwegian land. The war ended in 1660. Then in 1700, Denmark fought to reclaim its land. But after fighting for 20 years, Denmark was unsuccessful.

Denmark lost more land when it fought with France against England and Sweden. England won, and in 1814 Denmark and Sweden signed the Treaty of Kiel. In the treaty, Denmark was forced to give Norway to Sweden.

In 1848, the Danish **provinces** Holstein (HOHL-stine) and Schleswig (SHLAYS-vihk) **rebelled**. They wanted to break away from Denmark and join Germany. Denmark defeated the rebels. But in 1864, Austria and the German state of Prussia invaded and took over these lands.

Denmark's King Frederik VII adopted a new **constitution** in 1849. It made the nation a **democracy** with a two-house **parliament**. The landowners became very powerful in the parliament's upper house.

King Frederik VII

When World War I started in 1914, Denmark was **neutral**. After the war, the country regained Schleswig from the defeated Germany. During World War II, Denmark was unable to remain neutral. In 1940, German forces invaded Denmark. The Germans remained in the country until they were defeated in 1945.

After the war, Denmark joined the North Atlantic Treaty Organization and the United Nations. Though the country was powerful, its government was unstable. The Danes believed Denmark's upper house had too much power. So in 1953, a new **constitution** was drafted. It made the **parliament** into one house called the Folketing.

Since 1959, the country has been involved in many European organizations. But in 2000, Danes voted against joining the **European Monetary System**. They wanted to preserve the nation's independence and **culture**.

Today, Denmark has many of the same problems that most industrialized nations have. But, the Danes continue to work together to preserve Denmark's place as one of the world's best countries in which to live.

Queen Margrethe II has ruled Denmark since 1972. For more than 30 years, she has worked to preserve Danish culture.

The Landscape

Denmark is on a **peninsula**. It also includes 482 islands. The peninsula is called Jutland. It shares a 42-mile (68-km) border with Germany. Greenland is part of Denmark, as are the Faeroe (FAIR-oh) Islands.

Denmark's two largest islands are Zealand and Funen.

Denmark is bounded on the west by the North Sea. On the north, it is bordered by the Skagerrak. On Denmark's east is the Kattegat and Øresund (EU-ruh-suhn). And on the south, Denmark is bounded by Germany and the Baltic Sea.

Greenland has a diverse landscape.

Denmark's land is mostly flat, with rolling hills. However, the west coast of Jutland has sand dunes. And, high granite cliffs rise along the Baltic Sea. There are no mountains in Denmark. The highest point is Yding Skovhøj (EUD-ehng SKOW-hoy) at 568 feet (173 m).

Lake Arre is the largest lake in Denmark. It covers 16 square miles (41 sq km). The longest river is Gudenå (GOO-thuh-naw). It is 98 miles (158 km) long. It begins in central Jutland and flows to the east coast.

Denmark's climate is calm and moist. Winds blow from the west, across the sea. So, they have been warmed by the **Gulf Stream**. That means the climate is mild. The temperatures range from 32° to 61° Fahrenheit (0° to 16°C).

Denmark has made much of its land into pastures and farming areas.

Rain

Rainfall

AVERAGE YEARLY RAINFALL

Inches		*Centimeters*
Under 20		Under 51
20 - 40		51 - 102
Over 40		Over 102

North
West — East
South

Temperature

AVERAGE TEMPERATURE

Fahrenheit		*Celsius*
Over 65°		Over 18°
54° - 65°		12° - 18°
43° - 54°		6° - 12°
32° - 43°		0° - 6°

Summer

Winter

Plants & Animals

In its early history, much of Denmark's land was covered with forests. They were rich in animal life. But, the increase in human population and farming left little land for plants and animals. Denmark has created the Rebild Bakker National Park to help preserve its natural environment. It is Denmark's only national park.

Today, only about one-tenth of Denmark's land is covered in forests. Most trees are **coniferous**. Spruce and fir trees grow in abundance. There are

Denmark also has many wildflowers, such as this field of poppies.

also beech and oak trees. Heather and other grasses grow on Denmark's moors.

A hedgehog

Denmark's large herds of animals have lost much of their natural environment. As a result, these animals are dying out or migrating to other lands. Despite this, there are still herds of roe deer and red deer along the border with Germany. And there are other animals, such as foxes, rabbits, and hedgehogs, that can live in a small environment.

There are about 300 species of birds in Denmark. About half live there year-round. The others pass through on their yearly migratory path.

A red deer

The Danes

Most people in Denmark are Danes. There are also German, Jewish, and Polish **minorities** living in Denmark. Other groups include Turks, Slavs, Iranians, and Pakistanis.

The Danes speak Danish. It is the country's official language. It is closely related to Norwegian. English and German are the most widely spoken second languages.

The country's official religion is Evangelical Lutheranism. More than 400 years ago, King Christian III made it the country's religion. Today, about 90 percent of Danes are Lutheran. Others practice Catholicism, Islam, and Judaism.

Most urban Danes live in apartment buildings. In **suburbs** and in rural areas, most people live in single-family homes. The **social welfare** system ensures that no Dane lives in **substandard** housing.

Many rural Danes live in cottages similar to this one.

In Denmark, children study Danish, history, geography, mathematics, science, and social studies.

Danes eat four meals a day. They are breakfast, lunch, dinner, and supper. Dinner is usually the only hot meal. A famous Danish dish is *smørrebrød* (SMURRER-brurth). It is made of butter spread on thin bread and topped with various meats. Danish *kringle* pastry is also a popular mealtime treat.

After a hearty breakfast of cereals, cheeses, and eggs, children head off to school. By law, children must attend school from ages seven to 16. After completing this requirement, about three-fourths of the students choose to continue their education.

Some students go on to attend secondary school, called *gymnasium*. Students who complete *gymnasium* may continue to one of Denmark's universities. All students who are accepted attend free of charge.

Students who choose not to attend *gymnasium* have another option. Denmark has **vocational** schools that offer informal education. These schools teach students who wish to enter specialized jobs.

Adults may attend folk high schools. Folk high schools were an important part of Denmark's past. In these schools, peasant farmers learned how to **diversify** their agricultural production. They also learned about history, government, and literature. Today, these schools offer courses of various study and length.

After completing their education, Danes work in the nation's service, agricultural, manufacturing, and tourist industries. Workers pay high taxes to support Denmark's **social welfare** programs. Danes have insurance for accidents, injuries, illness, and death. All Danes may join these programs.

Traditional Viking costumes, such as this one, are rarely worn. Danes now wear modern clothes unless they are dressing for a festival.

Smørrebrød

Smørrebrød are also called Danwiches. They are a favorite in Denmark.

- thin slices of bread cut in half
- butter
- lettuce
- favorite cheeses, meats, and vegetables

Lay out two halves of the bread. Cover the bread with butter, so any moist toppings won't soak through. Cover the corners with lettuce. Top with as many toppings as you prefer, making sure none of the bread shows through. Many combinations can be used in smørrebrød. Serve with a knife and fork and enjoy.

AN IMPORTANT NOTE TO THE CHEF: Always have an adult help with the preparation and cooking of food. Never use kitchen utensils or appliances without adult permission and supervision.

English	Danish
Hello	Hej (HI)
Good-bye	Farvel (fah-VEL)
Please	Ja tak (YAH TAHK)
Thank you	Tak (TAHK)

LANGUAGE

Earning a Living

Most Danes that live in cities work in the service industry. They work in hospitals, shops, hotels, restaurants, banks, and the government.

The manufacturing industry is the nation's second-largest employer. Danes manufacture electronics, transportation equipment, furniture, porcelain china, and silver products. The largest manufactured products are food items.

Many Danes work in agriculture. Farmers work about two-thirds of Denmark's land. Most farms are small, family-owned operations.

Farmers grow wheat, barley, sugar beets, and potatoes. But

Tourism is an important part of Denmark's economy. Legoland is Denmark's second-most visited tourist attraction.

This farmer is feeding his poultry. Most farmers cannot grow crops in Denmark's infertile soil.

because the nation's soil is not very fertile, most farming consists of raising poultry, hogs, and cattle. Farmers then produce eggs, meats, and dairy products.

Denmark's fishers catch more than 2 million tons of fish annually. They catch cod, herring, and pout. Much shrimp is also harvested.

More than half of the nation's **petroleum** needs are supplied by its North Sea oil reserves. Most of the electricity is supplied by **thermal power plants**. Windmills generate about a tenth of Denmark's electric power.

Splendid Cities

Copenhagen (ko-puhn-HAY-guhn) is Denmark's capital and largest city. It was founded in 1167, and it has been the country's capital since 1445. Today, Copenhagen is Denmark's center of trade and shipping. About one-fourth of all Danes live in the area.

Copenhagen has beautiful **architecture**. Its buildings have tall **spires** or domed roofs. Some spires and roofs are **gilded,** and some are made of copper. The Børsen Building, or Stock Exchange, has a spire made from the tails of four dragons!

Tivoli is a pleasure garden in Copenhagen that opened in 1843. Its amusement park, musical concerts, dance performances, restaurants, and fireworks thrill visitors.

Århus (AWR-hoos) is Denmark's second-largest city. It lies on Århus Bay. Its people make ships, chemicals, machinery, beer, and tobacco products. Århus Domkirke was built in the thirteenth century. It is the longest church in Denmark!

Tivoli is Denmark's most popular tourist attraction. It provides entertainment to about 5 million visitors each year. That is nearly the entire population of Denmark!

Connecting a Country

Denmark has an extensive system of public transportation. Its people also get around on bikes, in buses, and in cars.

The country has a wide system of roads. All the roads are paved. Most roads also have bicycle lanes. Danish State Railways operates the train system that links **suburbs** with cities, and cities with towns.

Trains connect most of Denmark's areas.

Denmark has 260 miles (418 km) of inland waterways. The country's **ferries** are an important part of its transportation system. Ferries operate between Jutland and the islands. Ferries also connect Denmark with Sweden, Norway, and the United Kingdom.

Bridges are important in Denmark, too. They connect Denmark with its islands and other **Scandinavian** countries. In summer 2000, the Øresund Bridge, which links Sweden and Denmark, officially opened.

Denmark's international airport, Kastrup, is located near Copenhagen. Denmark works with Norway and Sweden to operate the Scandinavian Airlines System. The airline connects Denmark with other countries. Another airline, Danair, flies between Danish destinations.

Øresund Bridge is a 10-mile (16-km) link for car and train travel from Denmark to Sweden.

Government

Denmark's government is a **constitutional monarchy**. It is ruled by the **constitution** of 1953. Danes who are 18 years and older may vote.

Denmark's monarch is the head of state. But, his or her power is ceremonial. The monarch appoints a **prime minister**. The prime minister recommends cabinet members to the monarch, who then selects them.

The prime minister heads the cabinet. Each cabinet member heads a government department. The cabinet recommends other government officials to the monarch, who then appoints them.

Denmark has a one-house **parliament** called the Folketing. The Folketing has 179 members. Two come from Greenland, and two come from the Faeroe Islands. The rest come from Jutland and its surrounding islands. Members of the Folketing serve for four years and vote on laws.

Locally, Denmark is divided into 14 counties and 275 **municipalities**. Each has a council elected by its citizens, and a mayor elected by the council.

Denmark's citizens face pollution, unemployment, and the high cost of its **social welfare** program. However, they have a long history of solving complex problems with limited resources. The Danish government is working hard to preserve the country's quality of life.

Christiansborg Palace is home to Denmark's Børsen Building, Parliament House, and Supreme Court.

Time to Celebrate!

Danes celebrate many holidays. Some are familiar, such as New Year's Day or Easter. Others may be unfamiliar, such as **Constitution** Day. But, Denmark's favorite holiday is one that is celebrated all over the world. It is Christmas.

Danes call Christmas *Jul* (YOOL). They begin celebrating on December 1. That day, they light candles and hang **Advent** calendars.

In the middle of December, families get Christmas trees. The tree is kept outside until the night before Christmas Eve. Then, to surprise the children, the tree is brought inside and adults decorate it with lights, ornaments, and the Danish flag.

Children open small gifts every day from the first to the twenty-third. On December 24, families come together for Christmas dinner. They eat a big meal that often includes roast meats, vegetables, and potatoes. They also enjoy gingerbread and delicious spiced cookies called *pebernødder*. After dinner, family members sing songs and exchange gifts.

Opposite page: The Tivoli Boys Guard is a marching band that parades through Tivoli Gardens on weekends and holidays.

Leisure Time

Danes have many ways to spend their leisure time. Those who enjoy reading can visit **Scandinavia**'s largest library, the Royal Library in Copenhagen.

Denmark has a rich literary tradition. Denmark's most famous writer is Hans Christian Andersen. He wrote fairy tales. Several Danish authors, including Henrik Pontoppidan, have won **Nobel Prizes** in literature.

Danes who wish to study history may visit one of the nation's 280 museums. The National Museum in Copenhagen has exhibits from the Viking period. There is also a Viking ship museum in Roskilde.

Hans Christian Andersen

Sports are popular activities. Soccer is the nation's favorite sport. Since most of Denmark is surrounded by water, Danes like to swim, sail, row, and canoe. The Copenhagen Rowing Club was established in 1865. It is the oldest sports club in the world.

Denmark is one of the world's most progressive nations. Its people have come together to assure that no one is without food, housing, and insurance. Today, they continue to make the decisions necessary to keep Denmark a great place to work and live.

In 2002, the Denmark Quadruple Sculls team competed in the Zurich Rowing World Cup in Munich, Germany.

Glossary

Advent - the period beginning four Sundays before Christmas that is often observed as a season of prayer and fasting.

architecture - the art of planning and designing buildings.

civil war - a war between groups in the same country.

conifer - a tree or shrub that bears needles or cones and keeps its needles in the winter.

constitution - the laws that govern a country.

constitutional monarchy - a form of government ruled by a monarch who must follow the laws of a constitution.

culture - the customs, arts, and tools of a nation or people at a certain time.

democracy - a governmental system in which the people vote on how to run their country.

diversify - to compose something of several distinct pieces or qualities.

European Monetary System - a system for members of the European Union that replaces individual national currencies, such as French francs, with a single currency known as the euro.

ferry - a boat used to carry people, goods, and vehicles across a body of water.

gild - to give an outer layer that appears to be gold.

Gulf Stream - a swift, warm current in the North Atlantic Ocean. It affects Europe's climate.

habitation - the act of living in a certain place.

minority - a racial, religious, or political group that is different from the larger group of which it is a part.

municipality - a city, town, or other community with its own government.

neutral - not taking sides in a conflict.

Nobel Prize - an award for someone who has made outstanding achievements in his or her field of study.

parliament - the highest lawmaking body of some governments.

peninsula - land that sticks out into water and is connected to a larger landmass.

petroleum - a thick, yellowish black oil. It is used to make gasoline.

prime minister - the highest-ranked member of some governments.

province - a geographical or governmental division of a country.

rebel - to disobey an authority or the government.

regent - a person who rules a kingdom during the childhood or absence of the monarch.

Scandinavia - a region in northern Europe that includes Denmark, Norway, and Sweden.

social welfare - a system that provides organized public or private social services for the assistance of disadvantaged groups.

spire - a tapering roof or pyramid shape atop a building.

substandard - falling short of a legal standard or norm.

suburb - the towns or villages outside a city.

thermal power plant - a factory that uses a rising current of warm air to produce electrical power.

vocational - relating to training in a skill or trade to be pursued as a career.

Web Sites

To learn more about Denmark, visit ABDO Publishing Company on the World Wide Web at **www.abdopub.com**. Web sites about the country are featured on our Book Links page. These links are routinely monitored and updated to provide the most current information available.

Index